The Skyscraper

**PETER SLOAN &
SHERYL SLOAN**

Illustrated by Virginia Barrett

Every day the children went
to school. Every day they
went by an old house and
an old hotel on the corner.

One day there was a sign on
the old house. The sign said
that a skyscraper was going
to be built on the corner.

A week later, a bulldozer tore down the old house and the old hotel. A front-end loader scooped up the rubble. Then it put the rubble into a dump truck. The truck took the rubble to the landfill.

A few days later, a giant power shovel dug a huge hole. The hole was for the foundation of the skyscraper. Large beams of steel were put into the ground.

When the steel was in place,
huge mixing trucks came.
These trucks brought wet
concrete. The concrete was
poured into the ground.

Some weeks later, a large crane lifted steel girders into place. Then the workers joined the girders together.

Soon the frame of the
building was complete.
Workers began to put the
outside walls on the steel
frame.

Inside the building, electricians put in the wires. Plumbers put in the pipes.

When all this was done, the
carpenters put up the inside
walls.
The electricians put in the
lights and switches.
The plumbers put in the sinks,
faucets, and toilets.

Then the plasterers and
painters made the inside of
the building look good.
The outside was cleaned up
and a nice lawn was
planted.

A few days later, people moved into the new skyscraper.